Did Y...

DORSEY

A MISCELLANY

Compiled by Julia Skinner

With particular reference to the work of John Bainbridge,
Roger Guttridge, and Rodney Legg

THE FRANCIS FRITH COLLECTION

www.francisfrith.com

First published in the United Kingdom in 2010 by The Francis Frith Collection®

This edition published exclusively for Identity Books 2012 ISBN 978-1-84589-544-0

British Library Cataloguing in Publication Data

Did You Know? Dorset - A Miscellany
Compiled by Julia Skinner
With particular reference to the work of John Bainbridge, Roger Guttridge, and Rodney Legg

The Francis Frith Collection
Oakley Business Park,
Wylye Road, Dinton,
Wiltshire SP3 5EU
Tel: +44 (0) 1722 716 376
Email: info@francisfrith.co.uk
www.francisfrith.com

Printed and bound in Malaysia

Front Cover: **MAIDEN NEWTON, DORCHESTER ROAD 1906** 54563p
Frontispiece: **NETHERBURY, HAYMAKING BY ST MARY'S CHURCH 1912** 65068v

The colour-tinting is for illustrative purposes only, and is not intended to be historically accurate

CONTENTS

INTRODUCTION

We Do'set, though we mid be hwomely,
Ben't asheäméd to own our pleäce;
An' we've zome women not uncomely,
Nor asheäm'd to show their feäce:
We've a mead or two wo'th showen,
In the village,
At the tillage,
Come along an' you shall vind
That Do'set men don't sheäme their kind.

A poem in the Dorset dialect by Reverend William Barnes (1801-86).

Despite the intrusions of the modern age, Dorset remains essentially rural. From the deep valleys and woodlands, to the high chalk downlands with their ancient ridge paths, where it is possible to wander for miles with only sheep for company, to the lowland heaths where rare birds, butterflies, insects and reptiles live amongst the heather and gorse, this land is as English as anyone can imagine. Dorset is bounded to the south by a long coastline of great beauty and variety, and it is possible to walk along its whole length, following the Dorset Coast Path, part of the longer South West Way, from the fossil cliffs of Lyme Regis to the vast expanse of Poole Harbour.

Some Dorset towns were settlements when the Romans held power, but most of them date from Anglo-Saxon times, for this was the heartland of the ancient kingdom of Wessex. Old market towns such as Shaftesbury, Sherborne and Wareham still hold echoes of those powerful Saxon kings – Ethelred, Ethelbald, Ethelbert and Alfred – some of whom lie buried in the churches and abbeys that they endowed and cherished. Other towns, such as Weymouth and

Poole, grew up around shipping and fishing, many of their seamen venturing as far away as Newfoundland. The Isles of Portland and Purbeck, both really peninsulas, not islands, bear the marks of the quarrymen who have wrought out tons of stone, not only for local buildings but for distant landmarks such as St Paul's Cathedral in London. Yet these parts of Dorset bear their scars proudly, like battle honours rather than as a despoliation.

Everywhere you go in Dorset there are fortifications, from Iron Age hillforts to gaunt castles, which bear witness to conflict and turmoil in the past, but there are also glorious churches, the result of more peaceful energies. The residents of a hundred manor houses shaped the landscape with their ordered parklands and pheasant preserves; and every plough and woodsman's axe has marked the land in some way, for the history of all society is writ large across Dorset's lovely countryside.

MELPLASH, THE VILLAGE 1912 65063

DORSET DIALECT WORDS

'Bibber' – to shiver with cold.

'Blather' – an uproar, a noise, a fuss.

'Chippols' – young onions.

'Culver' – a wood pigeon.

'Limber' – slender.

'Maggotty' – fanciful.

'Tinklebobs' – icicles.

'Quilkin' – a frog.

'Thic' – that.

'Gurt' – great, large.

'Cassn't' – can't.

'Mommet' – a cute, sweet or good child.

'Wagwant' – a whining or naughty child.

'Thunder-daisies' – ox-eye daisies.

'Dumbledore' – a bumblebee.

HAUNTED DORSET

Bournemouth's Town Hall is said to haunted by the ghost of a soldier from the First World War, who appears there on 31st October to help himself to a drink of water. Rooms in the Town Hall are reputedly haunted by a ghostly cat, and phantom horses and carriages have been seen outside the building, which used to be a luxury hotel in the 19th century.

A golden coffin is said to be buried somewhere in the parish of Milborne St Andrew, but those who seek it are met with thunder and lightning, and the sight of a headless funeral procession.

Woolbridge Manor at Wool was used by Thomas Hardy as the setting for the Turberville ancestral home in 'Tess of the d'Urbervilles', where Tess spent her disastrous honeymoon with Angel Clare. The real Turberville family did once own the house, and their spectral coach-and-four is said to drive out from the manor and across the bridge every evening – it is only visible to those of Turberville blood, and a sighting of it foretells doom.

A number of ghosts are said to roam Athelhampton Hall near Dorchester, including a headless man, a hooded monk in a black habit, and a mysterious grey lady who vanishes through the panelling of the Tudor Room.

According to legend, shortly before Shaftesbury Abbey was closed by Henry VIII in 1539, the abbess ordered a monk to secretly bury the abbey's treasure so the king's men would not take it. The monk did so, but suffered a stroke and died before he could tell the abbess where he had hidden it. The treasure has never been found, and a ghostly monk is said to wander the abbey ruins, trying to find the abbess to tell her where it is. His ghost is said to hurry along Park Walk outside the abbey grounds and then disappear through the wall, presumably at a point where there was once an entrance into the abbey complex.

DORSET MISCELLANY

The massive sea wall and jetty known as The Cobb at Lyme Regis was created after the nearby harbour of Axmouth fell into disuse after a cliff-fall in the 12th century, and the only alternative was to extend the harbour at Lyme. Jane Austen loved Lyme Regis, and featured the Cobb in her novel 'Persuasion' as the scene of Louisa Musgrove's accident, when she fell from the steps.

Lyme Regis had a significant ship building industry in the past. Probably the most famous ship built in the town was the 'Revenge', commanded by Sir Francis Drake during his battle with the Spanish Armada in 1588, and later by Sir Richard Grenville.

LYME REGIS, VICTORIA PIER 1912 65043

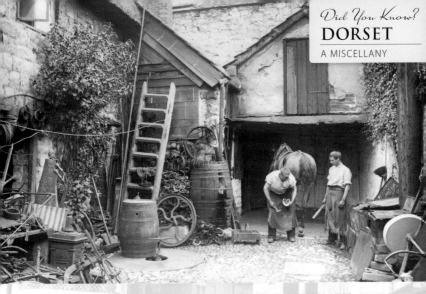

LYME REGIS, SAMUEL GOVIER'S SMITHY 1909 61633

The artist J M Whistler visited Lyme Regis in 1895 and painted the local blacksmith Samuel Govier at work in his forge. His painting, titled 'The Master Smith of Lyme Regis', now hangs in the Boston Museum in the USA. Photograph 61633 (above) shows Samuel Govier at work shoeing a horse in 1909.

The West Dorset coastline is so rich in fossils that it has been designated a World Heritage site, known as the Jurassic Coast. It was at Charmouth in 1811 that Mary Anning discovered the remains of an ichthyosaurus, helping to launch the new science of palaeontology and changing the course of scientific thought.

Inside the church at Whitchurch Canonicorum is the shrine to St Wite which still contains her bones. A stone coffin is supported by a base with three oval openings through which the sick inserted their diseased limbs in hope of a cure. St Wite was probably an Anglo-Saxon holy lady who lived in the area. In the later Middle Ages she became known as St Candida, now reflected in the name of the church.

CHIDEOCK, THE VILLAGE 1922 65078

In St Giles' Church at Chideock, the oldest of the peal of five bells
in the belfry bears an amusing inscription – when it was cast in
1602 the letters for 'Love God' were transposed incorrectly, and the
inscription actually reads as 'Love Dog'!

One of England's most eccentric events, the annual Stinging Nettle
Eating Challenge, is held at the Bottle Inn at Marshwood in west
Dorset every June – the brave competitors who take part actually eat
raw nettles!

At West Bay the River Brit is held back by a series of sluices and
released at low tide. The swell between the piers as the great waves
of Lyme Bay wash into the harbour entrance is an awesome sight.
West Bay became famous some years back as the location for the TV
series 'Harbour Lights', about the life of a harbour master.

For centuries Bridport was famous for the growing of hemp and flax and the manufacture of high-quality rope, twine and fishing nets, producing much of the cordage for the Royal Navy vessels as well as the rope used for the hangman's noose – the old expression 'to be stabbed with a Bridport dagger' meant to be hanged with a rope made in the town. There were formerly several flax mills around the town, and in the small streets and alleyways off South Street the old rope-walks can still be seen. The wide pavements of East Street and West Street in Bridport are said to have been constructed to facilitate rope and net making outside the inhabitants' homes.

In the early 18th century, Beaminster's economy was suffering because a hill on the main route out of the town to the north was too steep for the horse-drawn traffic of the time. The man who solved the problem was Giles Russell, a local solicitor, who was the main instigator of the Horn Hill Tunnel on what is now the A3066. The tunnel was opened on 29th June 1832 when a grand procession marched through it, a 21-gun salute was fired from the summit of Horn Hill, and fireworks were let off from the church tower. The people of Beaminster enjoyed the celebratory party so much that it became an annual event for the next fifty years or so, known as the Tunnel Fair.

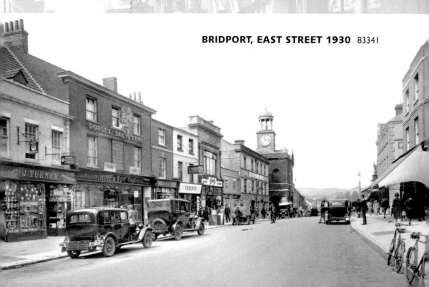

BRIDPORT, EAST STREET 1930 83341

Chesil Beach forms a line of shingle pebbles from Portland to Abbotsbury. A curious feature is that its stones are larger to the east than to the west. Between Chesil Beach and the mainland is an inland salt water lagoon, eight miles long, known as the Fleet. It forms an important habitat for diving and wading birds, and is often white with swans from the Swannery at Abbotsbury. The novelist John Faulkner Meade based his smuggling novel 'Moonfleet' on the now almost non-existent village of East Fleet on the shore of the Fleet near Chickerell. During a great storm of 1824, the sea came over Chesil Beach and engulfed the village, destroying all but 6 cottages and most of the parish church; all that remains of the church now is the chancel, which contains some interesting memorials to the local Mohun family.

PORTLAND AND CHESIL BEACH c1877 9614

Abbotsbury was once the location of a Benedictine monastery, St Peter's Abbey. Demolition followed its dissolution by Henry VIII in 1539, but its 14th-century Great Barn still stands, and gives an idea of the wealth that the abbey enjoyed – it is the longest ecclesiastical barn in the country. It was the monks from the abbey who established the original Swannery at Abbotsbury – in those days the birds provided a dependable source of feast-day meat. The Swannery is now home to over a thousand mute swans in the breeding season.

On a hill near Abbotsbury is a chapel dedicated to St Catherine of Alexandria, the patron saint of spinsters. It was the custom in the past for unmarried women to come here to pray for a husband with the words:

> *A husband, St Catherine!*
> *A handsome one, St Catherine!*
> *A rich one, St Catherine!*
> *A nice one, St Catherine!*
> *And soon, St Catherine!*

Did You Know?
DORSET
A MISCELLANY

PORTLAND, THE QUARRY 1894 34553x

Portland is famous for its stone quarries that produce a fine, white, durable stone renowned as a prime building material. Sir Christopher Wren used Portland stone for St Paul's Cathedral in London. In the 19th century, some of the work in the stone quarries was done by convicts from the prison on Portland, which was originally founded to provide convict labour for the construction of the breakwater of Portland's deep-water harbour, once a great naval base.

The area of Portland known as Pennsylvania was named by James Penn, Governor of the island in Napoleonic times, in honour of his grandfather William Penn, who was the founder of the American state of that name.

The coast off Portland Bill is a dangerous place for shipping. On one side of the Portland peninsula is West Bay and on the other is Weymouth Bay, and the place where the tide meets between the two bays as the deadly Portland Race. This area of very strong currents has dragged numerous ships, along with their cargoes and crews, to a watery grave.

Modern-day Weymouth was originally two separate medieval towns, Weymouth and Melcombe Regis, both of which developed as ports on either side of the mouth of the River Wey. The two towns were united in 1571, and the 'new' town took the name of Weymouth, even though Melcombe Regis had been the larger settlement. The first bridge was built across the harbour between the two parts of Weymouth in 1597.

Weymouth is the site of two old strongholds. Sandsfoot Castle, now ruinous, was built by Henry VIII to guard the sea-lanes between Weymouth and Portland. The Nothe Fort was built on a headland overlooking the Isle of Portland from 1860-73 to guard the huge naval harbour between the mainland and Portland. The fort was equipped with quick-firing guns and could accommodate a battalion of soldiers.

WEYMOUTH, THE SANDS 1918 68116

Weymouth was one of the earliest seaside holiday resorts on England's south coast, thanks to the royal patronage of George III in the late 18th and early 19th centuries, who came here to sea bathe on the recommendation of his doctors. Weymouth's loyal citizens employed a brass band, discreetly hidden in a nearby bathing machine, to play 'God Save the King' as His Majesty plunged into the waves. Fashionable Georgian society flocked to Weymouth in the king's wake, and many of the buildings along the Parade date from this period. In 1808 a large hill figure of George III riding on a white horse was carved on the hillside outside Weymouth near Osmington, in commemoration of his importance to the town. It was created at the bidding of John Rainier, a local worthy, and probably cut by militiamen stationed in the area.

The landscape painter John Constable and his wife Maria spent their honeymoon at Osmington near Weymouth in 1816. Constable painted a seascape during his stay, entitled 'Osmington Shore, near Weymouth', which now hangs in the Louvre in Paris.

The spring at Upwey was once famous for the healing powers of its water. George III often went there to drink the water whilst he was in Weymouth, and a special gold cup was kept there for him to use – it was later presented to Royal Ascot to be used as the Gold Cup trophy at Royal Ascot's race meeting. In Victorian times the spring was turned into an attraction for tourists by becoming a wishing well, which is still there, set in a delightful garden.

Many of Dorset's highest summits are crowned with Iron Age hillforts of the Durotriges people, the Celtic tribe that lived in this area at the time of the Roman conquest of Britain in the first century AD. One of the most impressive is Maiden Castle near Dorchester, which was stormed and taken by the Second Augustan Legion in AD44. A poignant exhibit in the Dorset County Museum in Dorchester is the skeleton of one of the British defenders of Maiden Castle with a ballista bolt from the Roman artillery embedded in his spine.

UPWEY, THE WISHING WELL c1897 34554a

DORCHESTER, HIGH EAST STREET 1891 28512

Beneath present-day Dorchester are the remains of the Roman settlement of 'Durnovaria'. The number of luxurious houses, many with mosaic floors, which have been discovered in Dorchester attests to the wealth of some of the inhabitants in the Roman period. In the Dorset County Museum in Dorchester are three Roman mosaics that have been lifted from their original sites and set into the museum's floor. Visitors sometimes express surprise that they can walk on such precious Roman artefacts – but that is what they were designed for!

The interior of St Peter's Church in High West Street in Dorchester is dominated by the tomb of Denzil, Lord Holles, who was the town's MP before the Civil War and fought for Parliament, yet later became a privy councillor to Charles II. Outside the church stands a statue of one of Dorset's literary 'greats', William Barnes (1801-1886). Born at Bagber near Sturminster Newton, he ran a school in Dorchester from 1835 to 1862, and ended his days as the vicar of Winterborne Came. Although he wrote poetry in standard English, he is most famous for his works in the Dorset dialect, which he loved and wished to preserve.

During the reign of Elizabeth I, fourteen Dorset people were executed for their religious beliefs; seven of the executions took place at Gallows Hill in Dorchester, which is today at the junction of South Walks and Icen Way. These tragic events are now commemorated with a series of statues on the site by the world-famous sculptress Elisabeth Frink (1930-1993) who used to live in Dorset.

In the 1620s, three groups of colonists went from southern Dorset to what became Massachusetts in the USA. As a result, a town of Dorchester was founded there – today it is a suburb of the state capital, Boston.

DORCHESTER, THE DORSET MARTYRS SCULPTURE 2004 D44706

Thomas Hardy, poet and novelist, was born in 1840 in the cottage in Higher Bockhampton shown in photograph H457086 (below). Apart from five years spent in London, Hardy lived here for almost 30 years, leaving in 1874 when he married his first wife, and he wrote his first three published novels sitting on the window ledge of the upstairs right-hand room. Before becoming a writer Thomas Hardy had trained as an architect, and on the outskirts of Dorchester is Max Gate, the home that he designed for himself and where he lived from 1885 until his death in 1928.

**DORCHESTER
THE THOMAS HARDY
STATUE c1965** D44101

Puddletown is the 'Weatherbury' of Hardy's 'Far From the Madding Crowd'. In former times the musicians of the village band would have played for services from the fine west gallery of the parish church; Thomas Hardy's own grandfather occasionally played there, and Hardy immortalised the antics of just such a village band in 'Under The Greenwood Tree'.

HIGHER BOCKHAMPTON, THOMAS HARDY'S BIRTHPLACE c1960 H457086

Many of the charming cottages around Dorset that we admire today would have been rural slums in the 19th century, when the Dorset agricultural labourer was the lowest paid worker in the country and living conditions in rural Dorset were notoriously poor. In 1834 six agricultural labourers in Tolpuddle founded a Friendly Society in a quest for better wages and conditions after their pay had been reduced from 9 shillings a week to 6. The men are now known as the Tolpuddle Martyrs, but at the time they were called the Dorchester Unionists. Forming a union was not actually illegal at this date but the local landowners were keen to stamp down on stirrings of dissent amongst the workforce, and the men were arrested and tried for the crime of making members take an 'illegal oath' during an initiation ceremony for their society – the banning of illegal oaths dated back to 1817, a time of suspected revolutionary activity, to prevent 'Seditious Meetings and Assemblies'. The six men were found guilty and were sentenced to transportation to Australia for seven years. There was a public outcry at the harsh sentences and a national campaign for the men to be pardoned; their sentences were eventually rescinded, and the men returned home to Dorset from Australia several years later. However, they found it hard to settle back in England and all the Martyrs except one later emigrated to Canada with their families. During their trial a written statement prepared by George Loveless, the leader of the group, was read out in court and was widely reported in the newspapers. His dignified words still resonate over the years:

'My Lord, if we have violated any law, it was not done intentionally; we have injured no man's reputation, character, person or property; we were uniting together to preserve ourselves, our wives and our children from utter degradation and starvation.'

SHERBORNE, THE ABBEY, THE NAVE EAST 1927 80329

On the hillside above Cerne Abbas is the famous chalk-cut figure of the Cerne Giant, often called the Rude Man of Cerne. The figure is of a nude man, with phallus accentuated; he holds a club, and may at one time have also held a cloak over his other, outstretched, arm. The origins of the figure are a mystery, but the most likely suggestion is that the Giant represents Hercules and was created in Roman times. The style of the Giant and his club are typical of Romano-British art, and the Hercules cult was popular at the end of the 2nd century. A local fertility tradition linked with the Giant was that a young woman who spent the night sleeping within the outline of the figure would be the mother of many children.

St Mary's Church in Maiden Newton has what is believed to be the oldest original church door in England, made in 1450 and still hanging on its original hinges. The village is also the home of one of the oldest fire-engines in the country, built in 1851 and still in full working order.

The Church of St Peter and St Paul at Cattistock is notable for its fine tower, its pinnacles and long vertical bell-openings increasing the illusion of height. Another feature of this church is an exquisite window by William Morris in which six angels, three clothed in shades of red and three in gold, stand against a dark blue sky scattered with stars.

Ryme Intrinseca has one of Dorset's most unusual place names. The 'Ryme' part means 'a rim' or 'edge of a ridge', signifying a settlement in a sheltered place. In the 15th century the lord of the manor held many other properties over a wide area; those near the Ryme manor were called 'Intrinseca', meaning the inside, or home part, of the manor, and the lands further away were known as Ryme Extrinseca (outside). Eventually the other lands were sold off, leaving only Ryme Intrinseca remaining.

Sherborne is one of the most historic and attractive towns in Dorset, centred around its beautiful abbey which is rated by many people as the most important piece of architecture in the county. The abbey is famous for its 15th-century fan vaulting (which in one place features a mermaid) and too many other treasures to list here, although the monument of Sir John Horsey and his son of 1654, showing the two men in the armour of almost one hundred years earlier, is particularly noteworthy.

SHERBORNE, LONG STREET 1924 75951

The word 'cheap' in a place name comes from the old English 'cepe' for a 'market' or 'fair' – so Cheap Street, as in Sherborne, meant 'market street'.

In Sherborne's Cheap Street is the Conduit (seen from Long Street in photograph 75951, opposite), which was originally situated in the cloisters of Sherborne Abbey and used as a washing house, or lavatorium. The Conduit was moved to its present location after the dissolution of the religious house and used as a market building. It has since served as a police station, reading room and bank.

One of the events in Sherborne is Pack Monday Fair in October each year. The name of the fair may originate from a celebration that marked the completion of building work on Sherborne's abbey in 1490, when the workmen 'packed up' their tools. Another theory is that although the fair was originally mainly a livestock market, it was also a hiring fair, when servants and farm labourers would present themselves for employment for the next agricultural year, which traditionally began on Old Michaelmas Day in October – so the name of the fair might derive from the 'pact', or agreement, that was made between employers and those taken on for work.

In St Gregory's Church at Marnhull is an amusing memorial to John Warren (d.1752):

Who smoked all his life
And so did his wife
And now there's no doubt
But their pipes are both out.

Woolland is a small settlement on the southern edge of the Blackmore Vale. Its present church was built in 1856, and a delightful feature of the building is a carving of a bird's nest – with the mother bird and three open-mouthed fledglings – on top of a pillar to the right of the east window. This was done by a stonemason to commemorate a robin that nested in the chancel during the building of the church; the builders halted their work until the eggs had hatched and the young birds had flown.

In the early 19th century a major industry of north Dorset was the production of a coarse white flannel cloth known as 'swanskin'; this hard-wearing material was particularly used for clothes for soldiers and fishermen. In 1812, around 1,200 people were said to be employed in Sturminster Newton alone in the production of swanskin. Flax was also grown in north Dorset for the production of linen, and a form of coarse linen called 'dowlas' was made around Bourton and Gillingham, used for making mattress covers as well as the traditional smocks worn by country people; those smocks would often be decorated with beautiful embroidery, particularly the pattern known as Dorset Feather Stitch.

Sturminster Newton was only ever a 'minster' town in the sense that it was granted to Glastonbury Abbey by the Anglo-Saxon King Edmund Ironside in the early 11th century. It used to be renowned for its livestock market, but the old market area has now been redeveloped. On the outskirts of the town is Sturminster Mill, where two undershot waterwheels were replaced in 1904 by a Joseph Armfield 'British Empire' turbine. The mill is open to the public on working days throughout the year, when visitors can see this interesting mill machinery in action.

Gillingham is Dorset's northernmost town. It was once the centre of the Royal Forest of Gillingham, and King John built a 'palace' or hunting lodge called King's Court on the eastern side of the town, which is recalled in the name of Kingscourt – only the earthworks now remain. Gillingham was once an important brick-making area – the Gillingham Pottery, Brick & Tile Works was in business from the 1860s to 1969 and produced a harsh red brick that was much used in buildings around the town, and also in the development of the burgeoning resort of Bournemouth.

On a minor road between Gillingham and Buckhorn Weston is one of Dorset's lesser-known gems, a tiny church with a thatched roof at the small settlement of Langham. Designed by Ponting in an Arts and Crafts-Gothic style, this delightful church was built in 1920 as a memorial to those from the hamlet who died in the First World War.

In the 9th century King Alfred the Great established a Benedictine abbey at Shaftesbury for nuns, of which his daughter Aethelgeofu was the first known abbess. After the abbey was dissolved by Henry VIII in 1539 the buildings were demolished, and all that now remains of what was once the richest and most powerful abbey for women in England are the foundations of the abbey church in a garden, fragments of stone in the museum and the abbey precinct wall down one side of Gold Hill, the steep cobbled street hidden away behind Shaftesbury's town hall that featured in a famous TV commercial for Hovis bread. Gold Hill is now closed off to through traffic but was once the main thoroughfare into the town. This was also the site of the town's sheep and pig market in the past, with animals being sold from pens created by placing hurdles between the mighty buttresses of the abbey wall. Although the quaint cottages on Gold Hill are desirable residences now, in the not so distant past this was one of the poorest parts of the town.

SHAFTESBURY, GOLD HILL c1955
S593056

MUSEUM

An important industry of Dorset in the past was button making, and the museums in both Shaftesbury and Blandford have examples of Dorset buttons in their collections. For about two hundred years from the late 1600s many women in the area made their living working from home at 'buttony', covering thin rings of sheep's horn or wire rings with pieces of linen and then stitching them in a variety of patterns and styles, with names like Dorset High Top, Dorset Knob and Blandford Cartwheel. Then a button-making machine was invented and demonstrated at the Great Exhibition of 1851. Almost overnight the cottage button-making industry came to an end, causing great hardship to those who had depended on it as a way of making a living.

The Cranborne Chase once stretched from Shaftesbury to Blandford to Wimborne in Dorset, Fordingbridge in Hampshire and Salisbury in Wiltshire, with the town of Cranborne as its centre. From the time of the Norman kings until 1830 the Cranborne Chase was an area reserved for deer hunting, and for fifteen days either side of Midsummer, when most of the fawns were born, the Lord of the Chase could charge 'cheminage' to all travellers through the Chase, as compensation for the disturbance they would cause to the deer. The vast numbers of deer on the Chase inevitably attracted poachers in the past. An inscription on a gravestone in the parish churchyard at Sixpenny Handley records that poachers would leave deer carcasses in an empty tomb there until they could be disposed of in safety.

The 'Sixpenny' in the name of Sixpenny Handley on the edge of the Cranborne Chase has nothing to do with money. The village got its name because in Anglo-Saxon times it was part of the Hundred of Sexpaena, an administrative area.

A landmark of north-east Dorset is the triangular folly of Horton Tower, on a hilltop between Cranborne and Wimborne. This was built by the local landowner Humphrey Sturt in the mid 18th century as a vantage point from which to watch the local hunt when he was too old to ride out himself. It now serves a useful purpose as a transmitter point for mobile phones.

In the hamlet of Manswood, near More Crichel north of Wimborne, is the longest single stretch of thatched roof in the country – it covers a long terrace of cottages known as The Buildings, and is almost 110 metres (120 yards) long.

The streets of Wimborne are dominated by its magnificent minster. The oldest parts of the present minster date from the mid-12th century. The central tower was part of the original Norman church, and the west tower was added between 1448 and 1464 to house a peal of bells. The minster church is dedicated to St Cuthberga, sister of King Ine of Wessex, who founded a nunnery here in AD705 which gained an international reputation, and around AD740 sent thirty nuns to Germany to help St Boniface convert the local tribes to Christianity. The connection is revived through the modern twinning link between Wimborne and Ochsenfurt, whose abbey was founded by one of the Wimborne nuns, St Thekla.

WIMBORNE, EAST STREET 1904 52475

WIMBORNE, THE QUARTER JACK 1886 19488a

One of the treasures of Wimborne Minster is its chained library, which dates back to 1686. It is one of the biggest in the country with over 200 volumes, the oldest dating back to 1343.

There are many fine tombs within Wimborne Minster, including the monument of Sir Edmund Uvedale (died 1606) showing him lying at an uncomfortable angle dressed in full armour. The Beaufort Tomb shows the alabaster effigies of the armour-clad John Beaufort, 1st Duke of Somerset, and his wife, Margaret, lying recumbent on their elaborate 15th-century tomb, their hands entwined. It was erected by their daughter, Lady Margaret Beaufort (1443-1509), who was the mother of Henry VII. John Beaufort was a grandson of John of Gaunt (a son of Edward III) and his mistress, later his wife, Katherine Swynford.

An unusual feature of Wimborne Minster is the tomb of Anthony Ettricke, 'the man in the wall'. After falling out with Wimborne's inhabitants, Ettricke angrily vowed to be buried 'neither within the church nor without it, neither above the ground nor beneath it'. He later relented and made peace with the townsfolk, but was anxious not to break his vow so he had a coffin made and placed in a recess in the minster wall, in a position which he felt fulfilled the requirements of his oath. Convinced he would die in 1693, he even had that date painted on it – only to live until 1703.

A much-loved feature of Wimborne Minster is the Quarter Jack, which has stood on the outside north wall of the west tower since 1612, and marks the passing of each quarter-hour by striking two bells. Carved by a Blandford craftsman for ten shillings, the Jack originally appeared as a monk, but he was repainted as a Grenadier during the Napoleonic Wars.

BLANDFORD FORUM,
MARKET PLACE 1900
B282303

One of the wonders of Dorset is the magnificent avenue of beech trees that lines the B3082 road a few miles out of Wimborne on the way towards Blandford. There are 731 trees, 365 on each side of the road for every day of the year, and an extra one to take account of the leap year. They were planted in 1835 as an anniversary gift for Lady Bankes of Kingston Lacy House, possibly Dorset's grandest house, to form an imposing approach to the northern entrance to Kingston Lacy park. The trees are now coming to the end of their lives, and the National Trust is planting a new belt of hornbeam trees to the outside of the current avenue.

Blandford Forum is famous as the best and most complete Georgian town in England; it was rebuilt following a fire that devastated the town in 1731 to a comprehensive design for the whole project overseen by the Blandford architect brothers, John and William Bastard. The impressive and grand town church, which the Bastard brothers themselves designed, was built between 1733 and 1739, seen in photograph B282303 (opposite). The 18th-century interior retains its box pews, galleries, pulpit and mayoral seat, and it is very unusual to find a church so completely Georgian and with fittings, furnishings and organ all of one date. The small structure seen on the right of the photograph is a combined drinking fountain and water supply for fighting future town fires – it is often called the Bastard Pump, after John Bastard who designed and paid for it, but its correct name is the Fire Monument, commemorating the fire of 1731. It stands 'in grateful Acknowledgement of the Divine Mercy, that has raised this Town, like a phoenix from its ashes, to its present beautiful and flourishing State'.

Milton Abbey at Milton Abbas was founded by King Athelstan (AD925-939), but all that now remains of it are the chancel, tower and transepts of the abbey church, dating from the 14th and 15th centuries. In the early 1600s, five-year-old John Tregonwell fell from the top of the huge tower of the abbey church. It was the custom in those days to dress both girls and small boys in gowns and petticoats and young John's skirts ballooned out around him like a parachute – amazingly, he floated safely down to the ground and lived on to the ripe old age of 82.

Milton Abbas was created by Joseph Damer, who bought the Milton Abbey Estate in 1752 and became Lord Milton and the first Earl of Dorchester. He employed Lancelot 'Capability' Brown to design a lake and grounds where the medieval town of Middleton stood, and he had the entire village dismantled and rebuilt further away from his mansion house next to the abbey church (now Milton Abbas School). The picturesque 'model village' of matched cottages is the result of his quest for privacy. Most houses are now single dwellings rather than pairs of semi-detached cottages as they were in the original design. They seem idyllic now, but in the past they must have been very overcrowded – it is said that 36 people once lived in one of them.

MILTON ABBAS, THE VILLAGE STREET c1955 M80011

**BERE REGIS
THE CHURCH
NAVE c1965**
B480033

The church of St John the Baptist at Bere Regis contains several features of interest, including 12th-century carvings of heads, one showing a man clutching his jaw, symbolising toothache, and two others showing men grasping their foreheads, symbolising headaches. These are on the arches cut into the south wall of the nave, and were probably done as a warning to the congregation of the evils of gluttony and drunkenness. The great glory of the church is its magnificent carved and painted oak roof, which resembles a hammerbeam but is actually based on tiebeams. It dates from 1475, and was the gift of Cardinal Morton, Henry VII's Lord Chancellor, who was born in the parish. The Twelve Apostles, a series of almost life-size wooden figures in 15th-century costume, peer down from the mock hammerbeams. In the south aisle of the church are the canopied tombs of the Turberville family, which Thomas Hardy described in 'Tess of the d'Urbervilles', in which Bere Regis is disguised as 'Kingsbere'.

The red signpost at a crossroads on the A31 road about 2½ miles east of Bere Regis, near Anderson, was on the route from Dorchester Prison to Portsmouth along which prisoners were marched after being sentenced to transportation to Australia. The procession would stop for the first night of the journey at Botany Bay Farm, down a side lane from this signpost, where the prisoners would be kept overnight in a barn, chained to a large post. It was assumed that the guards would be illiterate, so the signpost was painted red to show them where to turn off the high road to the farm.

South of Bere Regis is Bovington Camp, home of the Royal Armoured Corps and the Tank Museum, where many tanks and armoured vehicles can be seen, some of which date back to the original secret weapon of the First World War. In the museum is also a display of 'Lawrence of Arabia' material – T E Lawrence, famous for his part in the Arab revolt against Turkish rule during the First World War, was stationed at Bovington in the 1930s using the pseudonym of T E Shaw in a quest for anonymity. He lived at the nearby cottage of Cloud's Hill, now in the care of the National Trust. T E Lawrence died in 1935 following a motorcycle crash near Cloud's Hill; his grave is in the cemetery at Moreton, with a handsomely-lettered gravestone cut by his friend Eric Kennington, who also created the famous marble effigy of Lawrence in Arab dress which is in the Saxon church of St Martin on North Walls in Wareham.

Stone has been quarried in Dorset for centuries, and the Purbeck area is particularly famous for a shelly limestone that takes a polish, known as 'Purbeck Marble', that became very popular in the Middle Ages for use in tombs, fonts and decorative pillars in churches. In the 18th century Purbeck stone was much used for paving stones, especially in London. There were once extensive stone quarries between Swanage and Worth Matravers, where the quarrying industry is recalled in the name of the pub, the Square and Compass, a reference to the tools used by the quarrymen. There were also cliffstone quarries between Durlston Head and St Aldhelm's Head, where the stone was lowered by cranes onto small boats and taken to larger vessels waiting offshore for transportation away. The famous Tilly Whim 'caves' near Swanage, now closed to visitors for safety reasons, were actually formed by stone quarrying.

SWANAGE, FROM THE PIER 1897 40301

In the 19th and early 20th centuries, Purbeck's older quarrymen used to walk to work smartly dressed in top hats and long tailcoats, and then change into their working clothes when they reached the stone quarries. It was also a Purbeck custom in the past that when a quarryman came home after work, covered with fine stone dust, he would sit upright in a chair whilst his wife washed the dust from his face; if he had no wife, then a neighbouring woman would come in to perform the task.

The coming of the railway to Swanage in the 1850s transformed the town's fortunes, not only helping its development as a seaside resort but also allowing Purbeck stone from the local quarries to be transported away more easily than before. Swanage Pier is really a landing stage of immense proportions. It was originally designed to facilitate the export of Purbeck stone, and was then adapted to serve the paddle-steamer trade, which took tourists to resorts and beauty spots along the coast. It is one of the country's more unusual piers; its long neck does not go straight out to sea, but veers rightward.

Swanage's Town Hall in the High Street was designed in typical late 19th-century style, but the centre of the building is a 17th-century classical façade with intricate carving that was 'recycled' from the Mercer's Hall in Cheapside, London. The façade was acquired by George Burt, the nephew and business successor of the Swanage stone and building contractor John Mowlem. George Burt salvaged much unwanted stonework and ironwork from redevelopments in London and brought it back to Swanage in his sailing ships that had transported Purbeck stone to the capital, for re-use around the town – for example, the local landmark of the Wellington Clock Tower overlooking Swanage Bay was originally erected near London Bridge in 1854 but was considered a traffic hazard and later removed, and George Burt brought it (without its clock) to Swanage in 1866. On the other side of the High Street is George Burt's own former home, Purbeck House (now a hotel), which was also constructed using recycled materials that he had salvaged from London. The walls of this unique building are made of chips of different coloured marble that was waste material from the steps of the Albert Memorial in Kensington Gardens.

SWANAGE, THE GLOBE 1894 34607

LULWORTH, A STEAMSHIP 1925 78804

The giant Globe in the Durlston Country Park near Swanage is made of Portland stone, and is placed to represent the position of the Earth in space, with four stone benches nearby marking the points of the compass.

Moreton's church of St Nicholas is famous for the stunning series of glass windows that were engraved by Laurence Whistler from 1958 to 1984. The windows offer inspired interpretations of various forms and qualities of light, including candlelight, sunlight, jewel-light, starlight and lightning. Many are richly pictorial, depicting a variety of animals, birds and butterflies, buildings and landscapes.

The church of St Nicholas at Studland is considered to be the best and most complete Norman church in the county. The central Norman tower is preserved almost unchanged, and the nave and chancel are both rich in 12th-century features. The nave walls are of the late 11th century and have later corbel tables depicting human and animal heads.

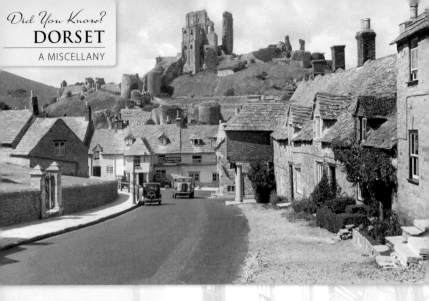

CORFE CASTLE, THE VILLAGE AND THE CASTLE c1955 C160015

Corfe Castle was built to guard the only gap in the ridge of chalk which separates Purbeck from the rest of Dorset. William the Conqueror began the castle in the 1170s, and it was much extended and enlarged over the centuries. The inner bailey contains the 12th-century Keep and a 13th-century house called the Gloriette, built for King John who used the castle while he was hunting in the area. The castle has a long and dramatic history, and was famously defended by Lady Mary Bankes during the Civil War. In 1643 she held the castle against Parliamentarian forces, personally defending the whole of the upper ward with only her daughters, her waiting women and five men; this makeshift force hurled down stones, boiling water and red-hot embers so successfully that the besiegers 'ran away crying'. She defended the castle again during a second siege in 1646, and only lost it through treachery when Parliamentarian troops disguised as Royalist reinforcements were let into the castle by one of the garrison.

In Wareham's South Street is the Rex cinema, the only remaining gas-lit cinema in Britain.

Wareham stands at the point where the Rivers Piddle and Frome empty their waters into Poole Harbour. The old town of Wareham lies within earthen ramparts (now known as Town Walls) that were raised for its defence by Alfred the Great in the 9th century. Nevertheless, the town suffered frequent attacks from the Vikings. In Saxon and early Norman times, Wareham was the main port serving south-east Dorset, rather than Poole.

Ball clay is a high-grade plastic clay that is found beneath the heaths around Wareham and is still produced in large quantities. In the 18th and 19th centuries, Dorset clay was shipped out from Poole to Liverpool to be sent on from there to the Staffordshire potteries, but in the second half of the 19th century it began to be used by the local pottery and tile works in Poole. The remains of an old clay working at Furzebrook is now one of Dorset's curiosities – the Blue Pool. This is an old flooded clay pit, and the water appears a deep blue or green colour, due to the minute clay particles suspended in the water diffracting the sunlight.

WAREHAM, THE OLD GRANARY 1954 W173055

A great fire destroyed much of Wareham in 1762, and many of the Georgian buildings in the centre of the town date from the rebuilding that followed. Dorset's great historian, the Reverend John Hutchins, was Wareham's rector from 1744 to 1773 and was away from home at the time of the fire – luckily, his manuscript was preserved from the flames by Mrs Hutchins, 'not without hazard to herself'. The memory of the fire is one of the reasons why the 'Chimney Peepers' check the chimneys and fireplaces of Wareham's pubs during a traditional event known as the Wareham Court Leet on certain evenings in November each year. A group of quaintly-dressed men visit the pubs where, apart from checking the chimneys, they weigh the bread served in the pub, taste the beverages on offer, and levy a fine on the landlord if the service is not to their liking. They are the Officers of the Court Leet, the form of local government in past times which dealt with civil and criminal offences and also carried out various checks on the town's goods and services. Wareham's Court Leet is a reminder of those old checks, although it is now a light-hearted occasion of much jollity.

POOLE, THE CUSTOM HOUSE 1904 52814

Poole developed alongside the finest natural harbour in England, and one of the largest in the world. Close to the quays at Poole is the 18th-century Harbour Office, once the Old Town House, a club for ships' captains. On the front of the building is an old sundial, and on the side a carving of Benjamin Skutt, Mayor of Poole in 1727.

The Town Cellars in Poole were built c1433 to house the 'commodities of the staple' – mainly wool awaiting export. The building is one of the finest examples of a woolhouse in England, although it was originally much longer. It was cut in two about 200 years ago when Thames Street was driven through it. The longer section now houses the Local History Centre, while a shorter section survives as part of the King Charles pub.

One of the iconic buildings of Poole is the old Custom House on the quay, now a wine bar and restaurant. The most famous smuggling incident in British history occurred at Poole in 1747, when thirty smugglers rode all the way from Kent and Sussex to 'rescue' a cargo of tea that had been seized by revenue men from their cutter near Christchurch. They tied up the town's night watchman, broke into the Custom House and then rode off in triumph with their cargo. The smugglers were eventually rounded up and hanged for the break-in, a number of murders (including the murder of two potential witnesses at their trial) and other crimes.

Medieval Poole's most notorious citizen was the sea captain and pirate Harry Pay. In the early 15th century he became a thorn in the side of the French and Spanish, who knew him as 'Arripay'. One Spanish chronicler described him as a 'knight who scours the sea as a corsair with many ships, plundering all the Spanish and French vessels he can encounter'. However, Pay's actions had grave consequences for his home town. Angered by his attacks on their shipping, in 1405 the French and Spanish joined forces and sent a small army of crossbowmen into Poole Harbour in five galleys and two smaller ships to attack the town as a reprisal raid. The people of Poole put up a stern defence of their town, removing the doors of their houses to use as shields against the crossbow bolts, but there were many casualties.

**POOLE, MANSION HOUSE, MARBLE COD FILLETS
ABOVE THE FIREPLACE, LESTER-GARLAND ROOM 2004** P72705

Poole's prosperity for many centuries was due to its involvement in the Newfoundland cod trade. Hundreds of ships sailed from Poole for Newfoundland each spring, returning with cargoes of salt-dried cod. The trade made Poole merchants extremely rich and thousands of people were employed servicing the trade in both Poole and in Newfoundland. The Mansion House in Thames Street, now a hotel, was built in 1776-78 by the brothers Isaac and Benjamin Lester, who had a large fishing station at Trinity, Newfoundland, and ran the biggest fleet in the trade. They celebrated the object of their success in their home by having two fillets of dried codfish carved in marble on the fireplace of what is now the Lester-Garland room in the hotel (see photograph P72705, above). There are reminders of the town's historic connection with Newfoundland in some of modern Poole's street names, such as Newfoundland Drive, Labrador Drive and Cabot Way.

Until the local government reorganisation of the 1970s, Bournemouth, Boscombe and Christchurch were in Hampshire. County Gates at Westbourne in Bournemouth stood on the old boundary between Dorset and Hampshire. The area is now a roundabout at the end of the Wessex Way.

Bournemouth did not exist at all until Captain Lewis Tregonwell built a holiday home in the middle of empty heathland, on the site of what is now the Royal Exeter Hotel. At that time (1810-11), Tregonwell's house was the only building, apart from an inn, on a wild stretch of coastline frequented only by fishermen, turf cutters and smugglers. Captain Tregonwell began to develop the area with villas to let out for holidays, others saw the potential of the area and followed suit, and Bournemouth was on the map. During the 19th century Bournemouth was specifically developed as a select resort for the well-off, but in the 20th century it opened its beaches to all, and is now one of England's most popular holiday destinations, 'the Queen of the South'.

In its early days, Bournemouth's planners sought the advice of the influential Dr Granville, a connoisseur of health resorts around the country. As a result, a large number of trees were planted in Bournemouth's pleasure gardens, following his recommendation that this would 'improve the air quality'. True or not, the belief that the many pine trees in the area promote a relaxing atmosphere is still current today.

BOURNEMOUTH, THE PIER 1908 61180

Bournemouth's mild climate made it popular with invalids in the 19th century, particularly those suffering from tuberculosis. One invalid who came to stay in the town was the author Robert Louis Stevenson, who wrote 'Kidnapped' and 'Dr Jekyll and Mr Hyde' during his three-year stay there. The house he lived in, Skerryvore, at the corner of Alum Chine Road and Robert Louis Stevenson Avenue in Westbourne, no longer stands, but a memorial plaque marks the site. However, Stevenson, whose health had been ruined, in part, by the excesses of his riotous early life in Edinburgh, found things rather dull for him in Bournemouth, complaining in a letter that life there 'was as monotonous as a weevil's in a biscuit'.

The Russell-Cotes Art Gallery and Museum in Bournemouth specialises in Victoriana and the building itself, East Cliff Hall, is a wonderful example of Victorian architecture. It was left to the town by Sir Merton and Lady Russell-Cotes, along with their art gallery and collection of items picked up in their travels all over the world. The museum also has a collection of theatrical items relating to the great 19th-century actor Sir Henry Irving.

In the 19th century the Prince of Wales, later King Edward VII, had the Red House on the East Cliff at Bournemouth specially built for his mistress Lillie Langtry; she lived there for several years. The house, in Derby Road, is now the Langtry Manor Hotel and restaurant. The hotel displays portraits of Edward and his 'Jersey Lily', and embossed into the dining room fireplace are Lillie's initials, E L L.

St Stephen's Church in the centre of Bournemouth is a magnificent Gothic revival church designed by J L Pearson, constructed between 1881-98 and considered one of his best works. Sir John Betjeman said that it was 'worth travelling 200 miles and being sick in the coach' to see.

Bournemouth people are happy people – and that's official. In 2007 a national survey by First Direct Bank found that 82% of people in Bournemouth were happy with their lot in life, making it the happiest place in Britain!

Christchurch is the most easterly borough in Dorset. In Saxon times the town was known as 'Twyneham', meaning 'the town between the streams' – in this case, the Avon and the Stour, whose waters empty into Christchurch harbour. The Normans began the construction of the beautiful priory church in the town in the late 11th century. It was named Christ Church, and the town came to be known as Christchurch as a result. After the priory was dissolved by Henry VIII in 1540 the impressive building was given to the town for use as its parish church – the Norman nave is the longest of any parish church in England. It is famous for its wooden Jesse Screen in the Great Quire; carved around 1350, this tell the story of the family tree of Jesus. There are also some interesting carvings on the wooden misericords and bench ends inside the quire. One such is a carving known as 'the Wild Man', which shows a nude male figure with a club in his right hand, rather like the Cerne Giant.

CHRISTCHURCH, THE PRIORY CHURCH 1890 25203

SPORTING DORSET

Dorset's best-known football club is probably AFC Bournemouth, nicknamed 'The Cherries'. The financial problems that troubled AFC Bournemouth in the mid 1990s led them to become pioneers, as Europe's first professional 'community club'. A trust fund set up by supporters took over the club on 18th June 1997, with the club 15 minutes from closure. Within five years the club was playing in its own stadium. Weymouth Football Club is nicknamed 'The Terras' after its terracotta strip. The club famously held Nottingham Forest to a 1-1 draw in the FA Cup tournament of 2005-06 and appeared on Sky TV for the replay at the Wessex stadium – which Nottingham Forest won 2-0. Dorchester Town FC is nicknamed 'The Magpies' after its black and white home strip, and is one of the oldest football clubs in the south west of England, established in 1880. Poole Town FC is nicknamed 'The Dolphins' after the dolphin on Poole Borough Council's coat of arms, and its mascot is 'Dylan the Dolphin'. Poole Town had a terrific season in 2008/09, winning both the Wessex Premier title and the Dorset Senior Cup, but the club was denied promotion because of inadequate ground grading.

The present Dorset County Cricket Club was founded on 5th February 1896 but cricket was being played in Dorset over 200 hundred years earlier – the earliest reference to the game being played in the county was an advertisement for a cricket match in the 'Sherborne Mercury' dated 9th May 1738 when twelve men from Dorchester challenged twelve men to come forward to play them at cricket at Ridgeway Races – the advertisement stated that the prize for the winning team would be twelve pairs of gloves, each pair to be worth one shilling.

Dorset is famous for its watersports, with Poole Harbour and the Weymouth and Portland area being notable sailing centres. Poole hosts Poole Week each year, one of the largest dinghy sailing regattas in the country. Weymouth Bay is the home of the Weymouth and Portland National Sailing Academy which is where the British Olympic Sailing Team trains, and will host the sailing events for the 2012 Olympic Games.

Dorset has produced something very rare in British sport – a Wimbledon singles champion! The tennis star Virginia Wade was born in Bournemouth in 1945 and educated at Talbot Heath School. She is most famous for her triumph in the women's singles at Wimbledon in 1977, the silver jubilee year of Queen Elizabeth II, but she had a long and distinguished tennis career, and was responsible for two major 'firsts' in the sport. In 1968, before becoming professional, she won the first 'open' tennis competition, the British Hard Court Open Championship at Bournemouth; as an amateur she had to refuse the prize money. She later won the first US Open tournament, beating Billie Jean King in the final. Off the court, another 'first' was in 1982, when she became the first woman to be elected to the Wimbledon committee.

Poole is famous for its motorcycle speedway team, the 'Poole Pirates'. Speedway was first established at Poole Stadium in 1948. The Pirates now race in the Elite League, the top tier of speedway racing, and have won the Championship a number of times.

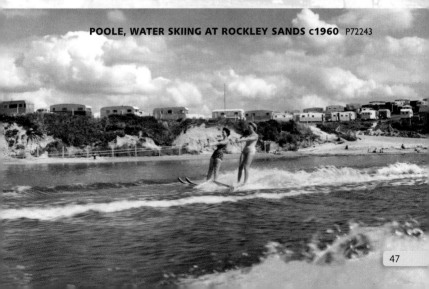

POOLE, WATER SKIING AT ROCKLEY SANDS c1960 P72243

QUIZ QUESTIONS

Answers on page 52.

1. The towering landmark of the Hardy Monument stands on Black Down above Portesham in south Dorset. Who does it commemorate?

2. It is considered very unlucky to mention a certain creature on the Isle of Portland – what is it?

3. Brownsea Island in Poole Harbour is a sanctuary for which rare and much-loved British creature?

4. What is the name of the railway line that runs through Dorset from Yeovil to Weymouth?

5. Thomas Hardy wrote a famous novel set in Dorchester, in which he disguised the town under which fictional name?

6. Which place in Dorset is known as 'the village that died for England'?

7. Which terrible calamity for England in the 14th century is believed to have been caused by a ship that docked in Weymouth?

8. What is Dorset Blue Vinny?

9. A 'yaffle' is a Dorset dialect word for which bird?

10. The oldest working letter (pillar) box in England can be found in Dorset. Where is it?

BEAMINSTER, A CHARACTER 1907 58145x

RECIPE

DORSET RABBIT

1 rabbit, jointed
25g/1oz flour
Salt and freshly ground black pepper
115g/4oz streaky bacon rashers
150ml/ ¼ pint dry cider

<u>For the topping:</u>
115g/4oz shredded suet
225g/8oz fresh breadcrumbs
2 onions, peeled and chopped very fine
Grated rind of half a lemon
1 teaspoonful dried sage
1 beaten egg
A little milk

Oven temperature: 180°C/350°F/Gas Mark 4.

Blanch the rabbit joints in boiling water, then pat dry. Season the flour with salt and pepper. Roll the rabbit joints in the seasoned flour so that they are coated all over, then place them in a casserole dish. Lay the bacon rashers on top of the rabbit joints, and pour the cider over.

Mix together the suet, breadcrumbs, grated lemon rind, dried sage and finely chopped onions. Bind the mixture together with the beaten egg and a little milk.

Cover the rabbit with the topping. Cover the casserole with its lid and bake for two hours in a moderate oven, then remove the lid and cook for a further 20-25 minutes, so that the topping browns.

RECIPE

DORSET APPLE CAKE

225g/8oz self-raising flour
115g/4oz butter or margarine
A pinch of salt
450g/1 lb apples
115g/4oz caster sugar
1 egg
1-2 tablespoonfuls milk
50g/2oz currants or raisins
A pinch of cinnamon or mixed spice, whichever is preferred
Demerara sugar to sprinkle on top

Pre-heat the oven to 180°C/350°F/Gas Mark 4.

Sift the flour and salt into a bowl. Rub in the butter or margarine until the mixture resembles breadcrumbs. Peel, core and chop the apples into small pieces and add to the mixture, and then add the dried fruit, sugar and cinnamon or mixed spice.

Beat the egg with the milk, and add to the mixture. Mix it all together well, forming a firm dough, and place it in a greased 20cm (8 inch) round cake tin. Sprinkle the top with demerara sugar, and bake in the pre-heated oven for about 1 hour.

This can be eaten either cold or hot, with the slices split open and spread with butter. It also makes a delicious pudding, served hot with cream, custard or ice-cream.

QUIZ ANSWERS

1. The Hardy Monument is not a monument to the famous author Thomas Hardy, but to Admiral Sir Thomas Masterman Hardy, who was Lord Nelson's flag captain on the 'Victory' at the battle of Trafalgar in 1805. It was to Admiral Hardy that Nelson addressed his famous dying words, 'Kiss me, Hardy'. Admiral Hardy lived in Portesham House in the village, and was a great Dorset hero in his time.

2. On Portland, rabbits are associated with bad luck, and it is still taboo to mention them by that name – they are referred to by terms like 'underground mutton', 'long-eared furry things' or 'bunnies', but never rabbits. The custom derives from the quarry workers, who thought rabbit burrows caused cave-ins, rockfalls and landslides and were thus a danger to them. The sight of a rabbit in a stone quarry was reason to pack up tools for the day and do no further work, as it was a bad omen. So strong is this superstition on Portland to this day, especially amongst the older people, that when the Wallace and Gromit film 'The Curse of the Were-Rabbit' was released in 2005, specially printed posters advertising the film had to be produced for display on Portland, with the film's title replaced with the phrase 'Something bunny is going on'.

3. Red squirrels.

4. The Heart of Wessex Line, also known more prosaically as the Bristol to Weymouth line.

5. Thomas Hardy's name for Dorchester was 'Casterbridge', as in one of his major works, 'The Mayor of Casterbridge'.

6. Tyneham, on the Isle of Purbeck, inland from Worbarrow Bay. In 1943 the Army requisitioned the area for training purposes in preparation for the D-Day landings and the villagers were told to

leave. They were assured that they would be able to come home after the war, and left a touching note on the church door: 'Please treat the church and houses with care; we have given up our homes where many of us lived for generations to help win the war to keep men free…'. In fact, they were never allowed back, as in 1948 the village was the subject of a compulsory purchase by the Army for training purposes, and it is now deserted and ruined. Tyneham is open to the public when the nearby Army firing range is not in use (usually at weekends), and is a moving place to visit. In the church is an exhibition of photographs of life in the village in former times.

7. In the Middle Ages there were two ports in the area now known as Weymouth, one of which was Melcombe Regis. A ship from Genoa anchored at Melcombe Regis in 1348 and carried the Black Death (a form of bubonic plague) to England, making Dorset the first county to be affected. The Black Death was spread by fleas, and would have come into Dorset by means of fleas either on the ship's passengers or rats that left the ship in Melcombe Regis harbour.

8. Dorset Blue Vinny is a cheese made in Dorset that was very popular in the 18th and 19th centuries. It is a blue veined hard cheese, made with skimmed milk. The popularity of Blue Vinny declined with the introduction of factory-made cheese, and the making of this cheese in Dorset died out in the 1960s, but has now been revived.

9. A 'yaffle' is a Dorset dialect word for a green woodpecker.

10. The oldest working letter (pillar) box still in use in England is in Dorset, at Barnes Cross near Holwell between Sherborne and Sturminster Newton (map reference ST 693117). Dating from the 1850s, the octagonal box has a vertical letter slot with weather flap and is cast with Queen Victoria's cipher.

FRANCIS FRITH

PIONEER VICTORIAN PHOTOGRAPHER

Francis Frith, founder of the world-famous photographic archive, was a complex and multi-talented man. A devout Quaker and a highly successful Victorian businessman, he was philosophical by nature and pioneering in outlook. By 1855 he had already established a wholesale grocery business in Liverpool, and sold it for the astonishing sum of £200,000, which is the equivalent today of over £15,000,000. Now in his thirties, and captivated by the new science of photography, Frith set out on a series of pioneering journeys up the Nile and to the Near East.

INTRIGUE AND EXPLORATION

He was the first photographer to venture beyond the sixth cataract of the Nile. Africa was still the mysterious 'Dark Continent', and Stanley and Livingstone's historic meeting was a decade into the future. The conditions for picture taking confound belief. He laboured for hours in his wicker dark-room in the sweltering heat of the desert, while the volatile chemicals fizzed dangerously in their trays. Back in London he exhibited his photographs and was 'rapturously cheered' by members of the Royal Society. His reputation as a photographer was made overnight.

VENTURE OF A LIFE-TIME

By the 1870s the railways had threaded their way across the country, and Bank Holidays and half-day Saturdays had been made obligatory by Act of Parliament. All of a sudden the working man and his family were able to enjoy days out, take holidays, and see a little more of the world.

With typical business acumen, Francis Frith foresaw that these new tourists would enjoy having souvenirs to commemorate their days out. For the next thirty years he travelled the country by train and by pony and trap, producing fine photographs of seaside resorts and beauty spots that were keenly bought by millions of Victorians. These prints were painstakingly pasted into family albums and pored over during the dark nights of winter, rekindling precious memories of summer excursions. Frith's studio was soon supplying retail shops all over the country, and by 1890 F Frith & Co had become the greatest specialist photographic publishing company in the world, with over 2,000 sales outlets, and pioneered the picture postcard.

FRANCIS FRITH'S LEGACY

Francis Frith had died in 1898 at his villa in Cannes, his great project still growing. By 1970 the archive he created contained over a third of a million pictures showing 7,000 British towns and villages.

Frith's legacy to us today is of immense significance and value, for the magnificent archive of evocative photographs he created provides a unique record of change in the cities, towns and villages throughout Britain over a century and more. Frith and his fellow studio photographers revisited locations many times down the years to update their views, compiling for us an enthralling and colourful pageant of British life and character.

We are fortunate that Frith was dedicated to recording the minutiae of everyday life. For it is this sheer wealth of visual data, the painstaking chronicle of changes in dress, transport, street layouts, buildings, housing and landscape that captivates us so much today, offering us a powerful link with the past and with the lives of our ancestors.

Computers have now made it possible for Frith's many thousands of images to be accessed almost instantly. The archive offers every one of us an opportunity to examine the places where we and our families have lived and worked down the years. Its images, depicting our shared past, are now bringing pleasure and enlightenment to millions around the world a century and more after his death.

For further information visit: www.francisfrith.com

INTERIOR DECORATION

Frith's photographs can be seen framed and as giant wall murals in thousands of pubs, restaurants, hotels, banks, retail stores and other public buildings throughout Britain. These provide interesting and attractive décor, generating strong local interest and acting as a powerful reminder of gentler days in our increasingly busy and frenetic world.

FRITH PRODUCTS

All Frith photographs are available as prints and posters in a variety of different sizes and styles. In the UK we also offer a range of other gift and stationery products illustrated with Frith photographs, although many of these are not available for delivery outside the UK – see our web site for more information on the products available for delivery in your country.

THE INTERNET

Over 100,000 photographs of Britain can be viewed and purchased on the Frith web site. The web site also includes memories and reminiscences contributed by our customers, who have personal knowledge of localities and of the people and properties depicted in Frith photographs. If you wish to learn more about a specific town or village you may find these reminiscences fascinating to browse. Why not add your own comments if you think they would be of interest to others? See **www.francisfrith.com**

PLEASE HELP US BRING FRITH'S PHOTOGRAPHS TO LIFE

Our authors do their best to recount the history of the places they write about. They give insights into how particular towns and villages developed, they describe the architecture of streets and buildings, and they discuss the lives of famous people who lived there. But however knowledgeable our authors are, the story they tell is necessarily incomplete.

Frith's photographs are so much more than plain historical documents. They are living proofs of the flow of human life down the generations. They show real people at real moments in history; and each of those people is the son or daughter of someone, the brother or sister, aunt or uncle, grandfather or grandmother of someone else. All of them lived, worked and played in the streets depicted in Frith's photographs.

We would be grateful if you would give us your insights into the places shown in our photographs: the streets and buildings, the shops, businesses and industries. Post your memories of life in those streets on the Frith website: what it was like growing up there, who ran the local shop and what shopping was like years ago; if your workplace is shown tell us about your working day and what the building is used for now. Read other visitors' memories and reconnect with your shared local history and heritage. With your help more and more Frith photographs can be brought to life, and vital memories preserved for posterity, and for the benefit of historians in the future.

Wherever possible, we will try to include some of your comments in future editions of our books. Moreover, if you spot errors in dates, titles or other facts, please let us know, because our archive records are not always completely accurate—they rely on 140 years of human endeavour and hand-compiled records. You can email us using the contact form on the website.

Thank you!

For further information, trade, or author enquiries
please contact us at the address below:

**The Francis Frith Collection, Oakley Business Park,
Wylye Road, Dinton, Wiltshire SP3 5EU.**
Tel: +44 (0)1722 716 376 Fax: +44 (0)1722 716 881
e-mail: sales@francisfrith.co.uk **www.francisfrith.com**